Welcome to Planet Reader!

Invite your child on a journey to a wonderful, imaginative place—the limitless universe of reading! And there's no better traveling companion than you—the parent. Every time you and your child read together you send out an important message: Reading can be rewarding and *fun*. This understanding is essential to helping your child build the skills and confidence he or she needs as an emerging reader.

Here are some tips for sharing Planet Reader stories with your child:

Be open! Some children like to listen to or read the whole story and then ask questions. Some children will stop on every page with a question or a comment. Either way is fine; the most important thing is that your child feels that reading is a pleasurable experience.

Be understanding! Sometimes your child might need a direct answer. If he or she points to a word and asks you to tell what it is, do so. Other times, your child may want to sound out a word or stop to figure out a sentence independently. Allow for both approaches.

Enjoy! This book was created especially for your child's age group. Talk about the story. Take turns reading favorite parts. Look at how the illustrations support the story and enhance the reading experience.

And most of all, enjoy your child's journey into literacy. It's one of the most important trips the two of you will ever take!

For Taylor Mirrione
—L.M.

DEADLY SNAKES

by Lisa McCourt

illustrated by Allan Eitzen

Hissss! It's a deadly cobra!

Will that gray rat be its lunch?

The cobra can't see the rat.

The rat squeaks. The cobra can't
hear the rat.
Most snakes can't see or hear
very well.

Does the cobra even know the rat is there? Yes. The cobra sticks out its tongue. The tongue collects the rat's scent, or smell, from the air. The cobra pulls in its tongue and takes the rat's scent into its mouth. The rat's scent is carried to a special smelling organ in the cobra's mouth. The cobra knows that the rat is there.

The cobra attacks! It bites the rat with its sharp fangs. Poison shoots through the fangs into the rat's body.

The poison kills the rat. Now the cobra will swallow the rat whole. All snakes have special jaws that come apart. Their mouths can open very wide in three directions. With these special jaws, a snake can swallow an animal five times as wide as its head!

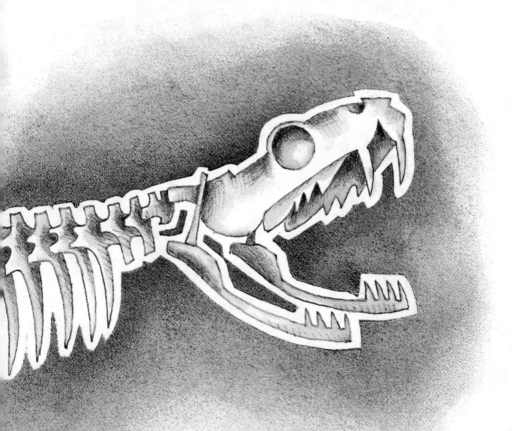

This anaconda has a different way
of trapping its food. It has caught a
young deer. The anaconda wraps its
body around the deer and squeezes
it. The deer can't breathe, so it dies.

Then the anaconda swallows the
deer whole. Look how big the deer
is inside the anaconda's body!
This anaconda won't have to eat
again for a very long time.

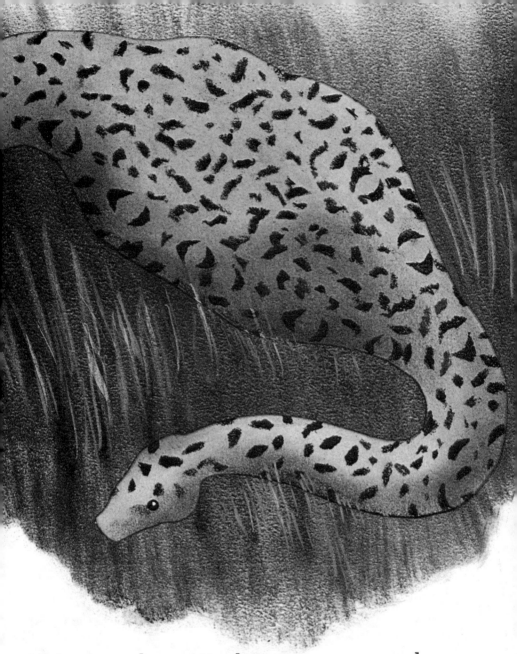

Most snakes eat about once a week.
But sometimes a snake won't eat for
a whole year after a meal!

Anacondas and pythons hunt mostly birds and small animals. But they can eat even bigger animals, such as goats, pigs, and leopards!

Anacondas and pythons are the
biggest snakes in the world. This
anaconda is as tall as a house! Most
snakes don't grow nearly that big.

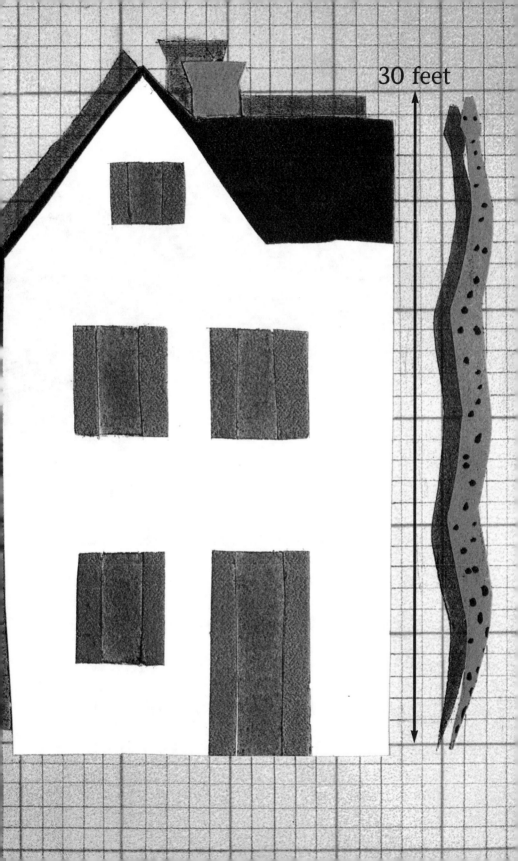

30 feet

When any snake grows, its skin
becomes too tight. The snake rubs
its mouth against something rough.
This makes the old, tight skin come
loose. Then the snake can slowly
slither out of it. The skin turns inside
out as it rolls off the snake's body.

The old skin is left behind in one
long piece. A shiny new skin is
already waiting underneath. A snake
can shed its skin two or more times
a year.

Snakes have no arms or legs, so they can go into very small holes and through narrow cracks. But with no arms or legs, how do snakes move?

The scales on a snake's belly are called scutes. They grip the rough ground and push the snake forward. If you put a snake on a piece of glass, it can't move well at all.

A snake's home is called a den. A hollow log makes a good den for a snake. So does an empty spot under a stump or rock.

A snake's den could be a crack in a stone wall or a space in a pile of stones. Sometimes when a fox or chipmunk moves out of its burrow, a snake moves in.

Snakes' dens help to protect them from animals that might harm them. But snakes have other ways to protect themselves too.

If a big animal comes near a king cobra's eggs, the snake will try to scare it. A king cobra will even attack an elephant!

Some snakes can rear their heads up high to scare their enemies. A black mamba can rear up as tall as a person.

Black mambas are also the fastest snakes. They can move as fast as seven miles an hour. That's probably faster than you can run.

This black-necked cobra *spits* poison at its enemy's eyes. It can spit as far as eight feet. The poison can blind its enemy long enough for the cobra to get away.

The hog-nosed snake is not deadly, but it sure can act scary! When it sees an enemy, it raises up its head and hisses. Its neck puffs out. It jabs its head toward the enemy, pretending to attack. But it keeps its mouth closed and never bites.

What if the enemy is not scared off?
What will the hog-nosed snake do
next? It uses its strong muscles to roll
over. Then it opens its mouth wide and
hangs its tongue out of its mouth.
It is playing dead.
This weasel does not want to eat
a dead snake. It runs away. The
hog-nosed snake's act has worked!

Some people are afraid of snakes, but this farmer likes them. That rattler helps the farmer. It kills mice that would eat his crops.

This scientist likes snakes. She uses their poison to make medicine.

Deadly snakes are dangerous, but
they can also be helpful to people.
And snakes are an important part
of our world.